POPULAR
POTATO
RECIPES

KÖNEMANN

Baked potatoes and fillings

When it comes to comfort foods, the baked potato in its jacket must rate as an all-time favourite. The basic cooking method is straightforward and the range of toppings and fillings can be simple or sophisticated, depending on what time and the occasion demand. Baked potatoes can be as substantial as you need; serve them as a main course accompaniment or a meal in themselves.

Baked Potatoes

Preparation time:
 10 minutes
Cooking time: 1 hour
Serves 2

2 large potatoes (660 g)

1 Preheat oven to moderately hot 210°C. Pierce potatoes all over with a fork; place directly on oven rack and bake 1 hour or until tender.
2 Prepare topping of your choice while the potatoes are baking.
3 Make one deep slash or a cross-cut in each cooked potato. Squeeze gently to open; spoon on topping. Or, scoop out the centres, mash with topping; replace.

Note: To microwave jacket potatoes, pierce all over with a fork. Wrap each one in a layer of absorbent paper and place directly on the turntable. Cook on High for 10 minutes. Leave, unopened, for 2 minutes.

HINT
Reduce baking time in a conventional oven by 15 minutes simply by inserting a metal skewer through the centre of each potato before placing it in the oven; the skewer is a most effective heat conductor.
For crisp skins, brush with oil, sprinkle with salt before cooking.

Baked Potatoes with a selection of toppings and fillings (see recipes overleaf).

Hot Chilli

1 teaspoon olive oil
250 g minced beef
1 small onion, sliced
2 cloves garlic, crushed
1 red chilli, sliced
1/4 medium red
   capsicum, seeded,
   thinly sliced
2 tablespoons tomato
   purée
1 cup beef stock
freshly ground pepper
2 large baked potatoes
chilli slices, extra, for
   garnish

1 Heat the oil in a
heavy-based pan; add
mince. Cook over
medium high heat for
about 5 minutes, until
meat is well browned
and almost all the
liquid has evaporated.
Use a fork to break up
any lumps in the mince
as it cooks.
2 Add the onion,
garlic, chilli, capsicum,
tomato purée and stock,
stirring to combine.

Bring to the boil, reduce
heat and simmer,
uncovered, for about
20 minutes. Add pepper
to taste. Slash potatoes
lengthways, top with
meat mixture; garnish
with chilli slices.

Spinach, Feta and Cashew Nut

15 g butter
2 tablespoons raw
   cashew nuts
8 large spinach leaves,
   chopped
freshly ground pepper
60 g feta cheese,
   chopped
2 large baked potatoes

1 Heat the butter in a
medium pan; add the
cashews. Cook over
medium high heat for
1 minute or until
golden brown.
2 Add the spinach and
pepper to taste, cook for
1 minute until soft. Stir
in feta. Spoon mixture
into cross-cut potatoes.

Black Russian

2 large baked potatoes
60 g smoked salmon,
   sliced
1 slice lemon, halved
2 tablespoons sour cream
2 teaspoons black caviar

1 Slash potatoes
lengthways. Top with
smoked salmon, lemon
and sour cream.
2 Garnish with caviar;
serve at once.

Soufflé Potato

2 large baked potatoes
1/2 cup grated Cheddar
   cheese
pinch nutmeg
freshly ground pepper
2 eggs, separated
2 sprigs parsley

1 Preheat oven to
moderately hot 210°C.
Cut tops off potatoes
and scoop out the
centres, being careful to
leave skins intact. Place
flesh in a medium mixing

1. Scrub potatoes well. Pierce potatoes all over with a fork for even cooking.

2. Bake potatoes directly on oven rack in a moderately hot oven for 1 hour.

4

bowl. Add cheese, nutmeg, pepper to taste and egg yolks; stir to combine.

2 Place egg whites in a small, clean, dry mixing bowl. Using electric beaters, beat until soft peaks form. Using a metal spoon, fold in the potato mixture quickly and lightly.

3 Spoon mixture into potato shells. Bake for 10 minutes or until puffed and golden. Garnish with parsley.

Swiss Melt

¼ cup cubed Gruyère cheese
2 slices ham, cut into strips
3 spring onions, chopped
2 large baked potatoes

1 Combine the cheese, ham and spring onion.
2 Spoon into piping hot, cross-cut potatoes so cheese begins to melt.

Spicy Prawn

15 g butter
250 g peeled, cooked medium prawns
pinch turmeric
pinch ground coriander
freshly ground pepper
2 large baked potatoes

1 Heat butter in medium pan; add the prawns, turmeric and coriander. Cook over a medium high heat for 1 minute, add pepper to taste.
2 Slash the potatoes lengthways and fill with prawn mixture.

Garlic Mushrooms

45 g butter
125 g button mushrooms, quartered
1 clove garlic, crushed
2 teaspoons finely chopped parsley
freshly ground pepper
2 large baked potatoes

1 Heat the butter in a medium pan. Add the mushrooms and garlic; cook until tender.
2 Stir in the chopped parsley and add pepper to taste. Spoon the mushroom mixture into cross-cut potatoes.

Napoletana

1 tablespoon olive oil
2 medium firm, ripe tomatoes, peeled and chopped
pinch dried oregano
freshly ground pepper
2 large baked potatoes
4 halved anchovy fillets
2 pitted black olives

1 Heat oil in a medium pan, add the chopped tomato and oregano. Cook for 1 minute. Remove from heat and add pepper to taste.
2 Cut the tops off the potatoes. Fluff up the centres with a fork. Place tomato mixture on top and garnish with the anchovy fillets and whole black olives.

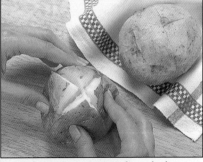

3. Make a cross cut in each cooked potato and squeeze the corners to open.

4. To microwave, pierce potatoes and wrap in absorbent paper, cook on High.

Side dishes and salads

Vegetable dishes are too often the poor relations in the cooking stakes – a great pity when their potential is, in fact, tremendous. Potatoes are the most versatile of all vegetables; they can be baked, roasted, fried, boiled and steamed to great success and team well with many other ingredients.

As an attractively presented side dish or a flavoursome salad, potatoes will always reap the compliments. Try our Almond Potato Croquettes for a special occasion, or Hot Pickled Potato Salad to pep up your barbecues.

Cheesy Potato Bake

Preparation time:
  25 minutes
Cooking time:
  40 minutes
Serves 4 to 6

*5 medium potatoes
  (1.2 kg), peeled and
  thinly sliced
4 spring onions, finely
  chopped
1¼ cups cream
1 cup water
1 chicken stock cube,
  crumbled
1 cup grated Cheddar
  cheese
2 tablespoons chopped
  fresh chives*

1 . Preheat oven to moderate 180°C. Brush a deep ovenproof dish with melted butter or oil. Cook the potato in a large pan of boiling water until just tender; drain.
2 Layer potato and spring onion in the prepared dish. Combine the cream, water, stock cube and half the cheese. Pour mixture over the potatoes.
3 Bake for 40 minutes or until the potato is tender. Sprinkle with the remaining grated cheese and all the chives. Return the dish to the oven until the cheese has melted.

Clockwise from top: Cheesy Potato Bake, Potato Swirls (page 8), Béarnaise Potatoes (page 8).

Béarnaise Potatoes

Preparation time:
 30 minutes
Cooking time:
 10 minutes
Serves 6 to 8

1 kg baby new potatoes

Béarnaise Sauce
*4 tablespoons water
2 tablespoons white
 wine vinegar
2 spring onions, sliced
1/4 teaspoon dried
 tarragon leaves
3 peppercorns
2 egg yolks, lightly
 beaten
150 g unsalted butter,
 cubed*

1 Cook potatoes in a large pan of boiling water until just tender; drain. Place in a serving bowl. Pour Béarnaise Sauce over potatoes just before serving.
2 To make Béarnaise Sauce: Place water, vinegar, onion, tarragon and peppercorns in a pan. Simmer, uncovered, until liquid is reduced to 1 tablespoon. Strain into heatproof bowl.
3 Place bowl over a small pan of gently simmering water. Whisk in egg yolks. Remove from heat. Whisk in butter, one cube at a time. Return the sauce to the heat occasionally to ensure it becomes thick and glossy.

Note: Béarnaise Sauce can be made several hours before it is needed. Leave, covered, at room temperature.

Potato Swirls

Preparation time:
 25 minutes
Cooking time:
 20 minutes
Serves 6

*4 large potatoes
 (1.3 kg), peeled and
 cubed
4 egg yolks
1/4 cup cream
1/4 cup grated Parmesan
1 teaspoon dry mustard
freshly ground pepper*

1 Preheat oven to moderately hot 210°C. Brush a 32 x 28 cm oven tray with melted butter or oil. Cook potato in a large pan of boiling water until just tender. Drain and mash.
2 Beat yolks, cream, cheese, mustard and pepper to taste until thoroughly combined. Beat yolk mixture into the mashed potato until thoroughly combined.
3 Spoon into a piping bag fitted with a star nozzle. Pipe swirls onto tray. Bake 20 minutes or until golden brown.

Potato, Onion and Tomato Bake

Preparation time:
 15 minutes
Cooking time: 1 hour
 30 minutes
Serves 6

*4 large potatoes
 (1.3 kg), peeled and
 thinly sliced
2 small tomatoes,
 peeled and thinly sliced
1 small onion, thinly
 sliced
30 g butter, cut into
 thin pieces
freshly ground pepper
1/2 cup milk
1/2 cup cream
1/2 cup chicken stock
1 cup grated Cheddar
 cheese*

1 Preheat oven to moderate 180°C. Brush an ovenproof dish with melted butter or oil. Layer the potato, tomato and onion alternately in dish, finishing with a potato layer. Dot each of the layers with pieces of butter and sprinkle with pepper to taste.
2 Combine the milk, cream and stock. Pour over layered potato. Top with cheese. Dot with any remaining butter. Bake for 1 hour 30 minutes, or until the potato is tender and golden brown.

Potato, Onion and Tomato Bake (left), Potatoes Primavera (right).

Potatoes Primavera

Preparation time:
  15 minutes
Cooking time:
  20 minutes
Serves 6

4 large potatoes
  (1.3 kg), peeled
  and cubed
60 g butter
1 medium onion,
  chopped
1 clove garlic, crushed

1 medium carrot, sliced
1 cup frozen peas
1 medium zucchini, sliced
1 cup halved cherry
  tomatoes
2 spring onions, sliced
freshly ground pepper
2 tablespoons lemon
  juice
¼ cup grated Parmesan
¼ cup pine nuts,
  toasted

1 Cook the cubed
potato in a large pan of
boiling water until just
tender; drain.

2 Heat butter in a large
pan; add onion and
garlic. Cook over
medium heat until onion
is soft. Add carrot, peas
and zucchini. Cook a
further 2 to 3 minutes,
stirring occasionally.
3 Add potato, tomato,
spring onion, pepper to
taste and lemon juice.
Cook, covered, over a
low heat for 3 minutes
or until heated through.
Sprinkle with Parmesan
and pine nuts just
before serving.

9

Tarragon Potatoes

Preparation time:
  20 minutes
Cooking time:
  8 minutes
Serves 6 to 8

*500 g baby new
  potatoes, cut in halves
2 egg yolks, lightly
  beaten
2 tablespoons sour
  cream
3/4 cup olive oil
2 tablespoons white
  vinegar
1/2 teaspoon caster sugar
1 teaspoon finely
  chopped fresh
  tarragon or chives
freshly ground pepper
2 tablespoons pine nuts,
  toasted*

1 Cook potatoes in large pan of boiling water until just tender. Drain. Cool.
2 Place egg yolks in a food processor bowl. Add sour cream; process until smooth. Gradually add oil through chute while motor is running. Add vinegar, sugar, tarragon and pepper to taste. Process to combine.
3 Combine tarragon mixture and potatoes in a serving dish. Serve sprinkled with pine nuts.

Hasselback Potatoes

Preparation time:
  20 minutes
Cooking time:
  45 minutes
Serves 6

*8 medium potatoes
  (1.8 kg), peeled and
  cut in halves
60 g butter, melted
1 tablespoon fresh
  white breadcrumbs
2/3 cup grated Cheddar
  cheese
1/2 teaspoon ground
  sweet paprika*

1 Preheat oven to moderately hot 210°C. Brush a shallow ovenproof dish with melted butter or oil.
2 Place each potato cut-side-down on a board. Using a small, sharp knife, make thin cuts into potato, taking care not to cut right through. Place potatoes, cut-side-up, in prepared dish. Brush with the melted butter. Bake for 30 minutes, brushing occasionally with butter.
3 Sprinkle with the combined breadcrumbs, cheese and paprika; bake 15 minutes more or until golden brown. Serve immediately.

Garlic Potatoes

Preparation time:
  20 minutes
Cooking time:
  45 minutes
Serves 6

*60 g butter
6 large potatoes (2 kg),
  peeled and cubed
2 cloves garlic, crushed
1/2 cup grated Cheddar
  cheese
2 tablespoons grated
  Parmesan cheese
1 tablespoon chopped
  fresh rosemary*

1 Preheat oven to moderate 180°C. Heat butter in shallow pan; add potato and garlic. Cook over medium high heat, stirring frequently, 5 minutes or until golden.
2 Transfer to a shallow ovenproof dish. Sprinkle with combined cheeses and rosemary. Bake for 45 minutes or until potato is tender.

HINT
The addition of fresh herbs to a potato dish can transform it from good to great in an instant. Experiment with different herbs and with spices. Small bunches of fresh herbs are readily available at greengrocers and some supermarkets.

Hasselback Potatoes (top left), Tarragon Potatoes (top right), Garlic Potatoes (bottom).

1. *For Perfect Chips: Cut potatoes into sticks 1 cm thick and 1 cm wide.*

2. *Gently lower the potato sticks a few at a time into the moderately hot oil.*

Cumin Spiced Potatoes

Preparation time:
  10 minutes
Cooking time:
  8 minutes
Serves 6 to 8

6 *large potatoes (2 kg), peeled and cubed*
1/2 *teaspoon ground sweet paprika*
2 *teaspoons ground cumin*
1 *tablespoon lemon juice*
1/4 *cup olive oil*
freshly ground pepper
1 *tablespoon finely chopped fresh mint*

1 Cook potatoes in large pan of boiling water until just tender; drain. Place in a serving bowl.
2 Whisk the paprika, cumin, lemon juice, oil, pepper to taste and mint in a small bowl for 2 minutes or until well combined. Pour over hot potatoes. Garnish with mint sprigs. Serve immediately.

Perfect Chips

Preparation time:
  25 minutes
Cooking time:
  6 to 8 minutes
Serves 4 to 6

6 *large potatoes (2 kg), peeled*
vegetable oil, for deep-frying

1 Wash and thoroughly dry potatoes. Cut lengthways into 1 cm thick slices. Then cut each piece into 1 cm wide sticks (see Note).
2 Heat oil in a deep, heavy-based pan. Gently lower the potato slices a few at a time into the moderately hot oil. Cook over medium high heat for 4 minutes or until pale golden.
3 Carefully remove from oil with tongs. Drain chips on absorbent paper. Repeat procedure with the remaining slices.
4 When ready to serve, reheat oil. Cook chips again, in batches, until crisp and golden. Drain on absorbent paper. Serve immediately.

Note: Potatoes need not be cut into sticks – thin slices or other shapes are just as delicious as the conventionally shaped chip. Potatoes may be prepared to the end of step 2 several hours ahead and stored in the refrigerator. Also, they may be wrapped and frozen for later use. For deep-frying, do not fill the pan more than two-thirds full with oil.

Perfect Chips, Cumin Spiced Potatoes.

3. Carefully remove chips from oil with tongs and drain on absorbent paper.

4. Cook chips again in small batches until crisp and lightly golden.

Almond Potato Croquettes

Preparation time:
  20 minutes plus
  30 minutes refrigeration
Cooking time:
  20 minutes
Serves 4 to 6

3 large potatoes (1 kg),
  peeled and quartered
1 egg, separated
15 g butter
freshly ground pepper
1/4 teaspoon ground
  nutmeg
1 cup plain flour
1 cup (80 g) flaked
  almonds, for coating

1 Preheat oven to moderately hot 210°C. Brush a 32 x 28 cm oven tray with melted butter or oil. Cook potato in a large pan of boiling water until just tender. Drain and mash. Transfer to a large mixing bowl; add egg yolk, butter, pepper to taste and nutmeg and stir to combine. Allow to cool.
2 Spread flour on a sheet of greaseproof paper. Spoon the potato mixture into a piping bag fitted with a large, plain tube. Pipe 4 cm lengths onto greaseproof paper. Alternatively, shape by hand into walnut-sized balls. Roll them in the flour; shake off excess.
3 Dip into lightly beaten egg white; coat with almonds, pressing them on firmly.
4 Place on prepared tray and refrigerate for 30 minutes. Bake for 20 minutes or until golden. Serve at once.

Creamed Potatoes

Preparation time:
  10 minutes
Cooking time:
  12 minutes
Serves 4

4 medium potatoes
  (920 g), peeled and
  chopped
freshly ground pepper
15 g butter
1/4 cup sour cream

1 Cook potato in a large pan of boiling water until just tender. Drain and mash.
2 Add remaining ingredients and mix to combine. Stir over a gentle heat to reheat.

Note: To achieve a slightly different flavour, substitute plain yoghurt, cream or milk for sour cream.

Potato Apple Cake

Preparation time:
  30 minutes
Cooking time:
  20 minutes
Serves 4

4 large potatoes
  (1.3 kg), peeled
1 large green apple,
  peeled and cored
1 small onion, grated
freshly ground pepper
1/2 teaspoon dried
  rosemary leaves
2 cloves garlic, crushed
2 eggs, lightly beaten
2 tablespoons olive oil

1 Preheat oven to moderately hot 210°C. Cut potatoes and apple into match-thin strips about 5 cm long; place in a large mixing bowl. Add onion, pepper to taste, rosemary, garlic and eggs; mix well.
2 Heat oil on a round oven tray in oven for 5 minutes. Spread the potato mixture on the tray. Bake 20 minutes or until crisp and golden. Cut potato cake into wedges to serve.

> HINT
> White pepper is more pungent than black. In a pale dish where appearance is important, use white instead of black.

Clockwise from top right: Potato Apple Cake, Almond Potato Croquettes, Creamed Potatoes.

Potato and Artichoke Salad

Preparation time:
  20 minutes
Cooking time: Nil
Serves 4 to 6

*500 g baby new
  potatoes, scrubbed
2 teaspoons finely
  grated lemon rind
1/3 cup lemon juice
1/4 cup olive oil
4 spring onions, sliced
1/4 teaspoon ground
  pepper
300 g jar artichoke
  hearts, drained and
  cut in halves*

1 Cook potatoes in large pan of boiling water until just tender; drain. Place in large mixing bowl. Add lemon rind and juice. Cover and cool to lukewarm.
2 Just before serving, mix in the olive oil, spring onion, pepper and artichoke hearts. Serve salad at room temperature.

Note: This salad is suitable to make the day before it is needed. Store, covered, in the refrigerator. Bring it to room temperature before serving.

Hot Pickled Potato Salad

Preparation time:
  20 minutes
Cooking time: Nil
Serves 6

*12 small potatoes
  (1.7 kg), peeled
  and cubed
1 small onion, finely
  chopped
125 g hot salami,
  chopped
1 cup chopped, mixed,
  pickled vegetables
  (see Note)
1/4 cup chopped green
  or black olives
1/2 cup mayonnaise
1/2 cup sour cream
freshly ground pepper*

1 Cook potato in large pan of boiling water until just tender. Drain; place in a large bowl.
2 Stir in all the remaining ingredients, adding pepper to taste. Mix lightly to coat. Serve hot as a main course accompaniment.

Note: A good variety of pickled vegetables is available in jars from supermarkets. They are also sold loose by weight at delicatessens. Choose a mixture of colours and textures.

Potato and Artichoke Salad (top), Hot Pickled Potato Salad (bottom).

Continental Salad

Preparation time:
  25 minutes plus
  1 hour standing
Cooking time: Nil
Serves 4

8 medium potatoes
  (1.8 kg), peeled
3/4 cup dry white wine
1/3 cup olive oil
1/3 cup lemon juice
freshly ground pepper
1 large onion, thinly
  sliced
lettuce leaves, to serve
3 hard-boiled eggs,
  sliced
chopped fresh parsley,
  for garnish

1 Cook potatoes in large pan of boiling water until just tender; drain. Cut into slices. Whisk wine, oil, lemon juice and pepper to taste in a small bowl for 2 minutes or until well combined.
2 Put a layer of warm potato slices into a mixing bowl, spoon some of the dressing over, top with some of the onion slices. Continue layering until all potatoes, onion and dressing are used. Cover, leave at room temperature for 1 hour.
3 Just before serving, line a salad bowl with lettuce leaves, spoon in the potato mixture.

4 Garnish with the slices of hard-boiled egg and sprinkle with chopped parsley.

Potato and Coriander Salad

Preparation time:
  25 minutes
Cooking time: Nil
Serves 4 to 6

6 large potatoes (2 kg),
  peeled and cut into
  thick slices
1/2 cup white wine
  vinegar
1/3 cup olive oil
1 clove garlic, crushed
1 tablespoon finely
  shredded fresh ginger
1 teaspoon finely sliced
  fresh red chilli
1/2 cup chopped fresh
  coriander

1 Cook potato slices in a large pan of boiling water until just tender; drain and place in bowl.
2 Whisk vinegar, oil, garlic, ginger and chilli in small bowl until well combined. Pour mixture over potato, top with coriander. Serve immediately.

Note: The dressing can be made several days ahead and stored in an airtight jar in the fridge.

Potato Pumpkin Salad

Preparation time:
  25 minutes
Cooking time: Nil
Serves 4 to 6

500 g pumpkin, cubed
4 small potatoes
  (560 g), peeled
  and cubed
6 spring onions, sliced
3/4 cup pecan nuts
3 sticks celery,
  diagonally sliced
1/4 cup chopped fresh
  parsley
1/2 cup mayonnaise
1/2 cup sour cream
1 teaspoon Dijon
  mustard
freshly ground pepper

1 Boil pumpkin and potato until just tender; drain, cool and refrigerate.
2 Place the pumpkin, potato, spring onion, pecans, celery and parsley in salad bowl. Beat mayonnaise, sour cream, mustard and pepper to taste in a small bowl for 2 minutes or until well combined. Drizzle over salad. Toss thoroughly to coat.

Note: Use dill in place of parsley, if preferred.

Clockwise from top: Continental Salad, Potato and Coriander Salad, Potato Pumpkin Salad.

Spiced Potato Salad

Preparation time:
  30 minutes
Cooking time: Nil
Serves 6 to 8

6 *small potatoes*
  (840 g), peeled
  and cubed
2 *tablespoons olive oil*
4 *rashers bacon,*
  chopped
2 *medium onions,*
  grated
2 *teaspoons curry*
  powder
1 *clove garlic, crushed*
2 *medium tomatoes,*
  peeled and chopped
1 *tablespoon chopped*
  fresh mint
freshly ground pepper

1 Cook potato in large pan of boiling water until just tender; drain.
2 Heat oil in medium, heavy-based pan; add potato. Cook over medium high heat until lightly browned. Drain on absorbent paper.
3 Pour oil from pan, leaving 1 tablespoon. Add bacon, onion and curry powder. Cook 2 minutes over medium heat, stirring constantly. Add the garlic and cook 1 to 2 minutes more. Return potato to the pan and heat through.

4 Add chopped tomato and cook gently to heat through. Stir in mint and pepper to taste. Transfer to a serving bowl, serve warm.

Potato Apple Salad

Preparation time:
  25 minutes
Cooking time: Nil
Serves 6 to 8

6 *large potatoes (2 kg),*
  peeled
1/3 *cup lemon juice*
2 *tablespoons olive oil*
1/4 *teaspoon ground*
  white pepper
1/2 *cup mayonnaise*
1/4 *cup sour cream*
2 *tablespoons*
  evaporated milk
2 *small, thin-skinned*
  cucumbers, cubed
1 *tablespoon chopped*
  fresh chives
1 *tablespoon chopped*
  fresh parsley
lettuce leaves, to serve
2 *medium red apples*
chopped walnuts, for
  garnish

1 Cook potato in boiling water until just tender; drain and cut into large cubes. Place in large mixing bowl. Place lemon juice, oil and pepper in a small jar. Shake vigorously

until well combined. Pour over potato. Toss lightly, cover and refrigerate.
2 Just before serving, combine mayonnaise, sour cream and evaporated milk. Pour over potato. Add cucumber, chives and parsley, toss lightly.
3 Transfer to a serving bowl lined with lettuce leaves. Core the apples,

Clockwise from top: Potato Apple Salad, Potato Bacon Salad, Spiced Potato Salad.

cut into quarters or eighths and arrange on top. Scatter with the chopped walnuts.

Potato Bacon Salad

Preparation time:
  25 minutes
Cooking time: Nil
Serves 6 to 8

1 tablespoon olive oil
3 rashers bacon
6 small potatoes
  (840 g), peeled
  and cubed
8 spring onions,
  chopped
2 tablespoons chopped
  black or stuffed olives
2 tablespoons chopped
  parsley
1/2 cup French dressing
1 tablespoon chopped
  capers

1 Heat the oil in a medium pan; add the chopped bacon. Cook over medium high heat until crisp and golden brown. Remove; drain on absorbent paper.
2 Cook the potato in a large pan of boiling water until just tender; drain. Place in a serving bowl with all the remaining ingredients, toss gently to combine.

Super starters

Potatoes may not immediately spring to mind as the stuff of which starters are made, but a quick look through the recipes featured here will definitely change all that. There are fritters and dips, pastries and pikelets, soups and chowders – an exciting variety of hot and cold items that will get any meal off to a great start.

To make things easy for the busy cook who is planning a special meal, some of the recipes have been created so that they can be prepared either fully or partially a day or two ahead. Others can be frozen for up to four weeks.

Potato and Cheese Cakes with Apple

Preparation time:
  25 minutes
Cooking time:
  10 minutes
Makes 18

2 cups mashed potato
  (600 g raw potato)
125 g Cheddar cheese,
  grated
2 tablespoons plain
  flour
1 egg, lightly beaten
1/2 teaspoon ground
  nutmeg
1 tablespoon olive oil

Apple Sauce
2 large green apples,
  peeled and cored
2 tablespoons water
2 tablespoons chopped
  fresh mint
1 tablespoon white
  vinegar

1 Combine the mashed potato, cheese, sifted flour, egg and nutmeg in a medium mixing bowl. Stir with wooden spoon until the mixture is just combined; do not overbeat.
2 Heat oil in medium, heavy-based pan. Spoon level tablespoons of potato mixture into pan.

Clockwise from top left: Seafood Mornay with Creamy Potato Topping (page 24), Potato Puffs (page 25), Potato and Cheese Cakes with Apple.

Cook over medium high heat for 5 minutes on each side, or until golden brown and cooked through.

Top each potato cake with a spoonful of Apple Sauce and serve immediately.

3 To make Apple Sauce: Cut apples into large cubes and place in a small pan. Add the water, cover and cook over low heat until apples are tender and all the water has evaporated. Mash with a fork, add mint and vinegar, stir to combine.

Note: Potato Cakes are not suitable for freezing but they can be made up to 2 days ahead and stored, covered, in the refrigerator. Reheat them in a slow 150°C oven just before serving. Apple Sauce can be made 5 days ahead and stored, covered, in the fridge.

Seafood Mornay with Creamy Potato Topping

Preparation time:
  40 minutes
Cooking time:
  10 minutes
Serves 4 to 6

1/2 cup dry white wine
2 spring onions, chopped
2 bay leaves
1 strip of lemon rind
500 g scallops
300 g large green prawns, peeled
30 g butter
3 tablespoons plain flour
1 cup milk

Potato Topping
6 large potatoes (2 kg), peeled
60 g butter
3/4 cup cream
1/4 teaspoon nutmeg
1/2 cup flaked almonds

1 Preheat oven to moderate 180°C. Brush six half-cup capacity or one 3-cup capacity ovenproof dish with melted butter or oil.

2 Place white wine, spring onion, bay leaves and lemon rind in a medium pan, bring slowly to the boil. Reduce heat, add scallops and prawns and simmer for 2 to 3 minutes. Remove seafood using slotted spoon. Set aside.

3 Bring the white wine mixture back to the boil and simmer, uncovered, until reduced to 1/2 cup. Strain; set aside.

4 Heat butter in medium pan; add flour. Stir over low heat 2 minutes or until flour mixture is lightly golden. Gradually add milk and reduced wine mixture; stir constantly over a medium heat for 4 minutes or until the mixture boils and

1. For Seafood Mornay: Add scallops and prawns to wine mixture. Cook 3 minutes.

2. Simmer the wine mixture until reduced to half a cup. Strain; set aside.

thickens; boil further 1 minute. Remove pan from heat.

5 Carefully stir in the scallops and prawns. Pour the mixture evenly into the prepared dishes.

6 Spread Potato Topping evenly over seafood mixture, sprinkle with almonds. Bake 10 minutes or until the potato and almonds are golden brown and heated through.

7 To prepare Potato Topping: Cook the potatoes in a large pan of boiling water until just tender; drain and mash. Add the butter, cream and nutmeg; beat the mixture with a wooden spoon until it is light and fluffy.

Note: The Seafood Mornay can be cooked a day ahead and stored, covered, in the refrigerator. It is not suitable for freezing.

Potato Puffs

Preparation time:
  30 minutes
Cooking time:
  3 minutes
Serves 4 to 6

60 g butter
½ cup water
½ cup plain flour
2 eggs, lightly beaten
¾ cup mashed potato
  (225 g raw potato)
¼ teaspoon chilli
  powder
oil, for deep-frying
½ cup grated Parmesan
  cheese

1 Combine butter and water in medium pan. Stir over low heat until butter has melted; do not boil.

2 Remove from heat, add sifted flour all at once. Beat until smooth using a wooden spoon. Return to the heat; heat, stirring, until the mixture thickens and comes away from side and base of pan. Remove from heat. Cool slightly.

3 Transfer mixture to large mixing bowl. Add eggs gradually, beating well after each addition. Beat until mixture is glossy. Using a large metal spoon, fold in the mashed potato and chilli powder.

4 Heat oil in a deep, heavy-based pan. Gently lower teaspoonfuls of mixture into moderately hot oil. Cook over medium high heat 3 minutes or until golden brown and cooked through. Drain on absorbent paper. Serve with Parmesan.

Note: Warm mashed potato is easier to work with, resulting in a smoother paste. Puffs are best served at once; keep warm only briefly in a slow 150°C oven.

3. Spoon the seafood mixture into the lightly greased ovenproof dish or dishes.

4. Spread the prepared potato topping evenly over the seafood mixture.

Potato and Herb Fritters

Preparation time:
  25 minutes
Cooking time: 8 minutes
Serves 4 to 6

4 cups finely grated
  peeled potato (660 g)
1½ cups peeled, finely
  grated orange sweet
  potato (350 g)
¼ cup finely chopped
  fresh chives
1 tablespoon finely
  chopped fresh oregano
2 tablespoons finely
  chopped fresh parsley
2 eggs, lightly beaten
¼ cup plain flour
1 tablespoon olive oil
1 cup light sour cream
fresh dill sprigs, for
  garnish

1 Combine potato,
sweet potato, chives,
oregano, parsley, eggs
and sifted flour in
medium mixing bowl.
Stir, using a wooden
spoon, until ingredients
are just combined.
2 Heat oil in medium,
heavy-based pan. Spoon
heaped tablespoonfuls
of mixture into pan.
Cook over medium
high heat for 4 minutes
each side or until
golden brown and
vegetables are tender.
3 Serve Fritters warm,
topped with sour cream
and sprigs of dill.

Crispy Skins

Preparation time:
  15 minutes
Cooking time:
  1 hour 35 minutes
Serves 6

6 medium potatoes
  (1.4 kg)
¼ cup olive oil

Filling
1 teaspoon olive oil
3 rashers bacon, finely
  chopped
1 medium onion, finely
  chopped
1 clove garlic, crushed
1 cup sour cream
2 tablespoons chopped
  fresh chives
freshly ground pepper
¼ cup grated Parmesan
  cheese

1 Preheat oven to
moderate 180°C. Prick
the potatoes all over
with a fork. Place on a
baking tray. Bake for
45 minutes or until
tender.
2 Cut each potato in
half. Using a metal
spoon, scoop out
potato flesh and place
in a large mixing bowl.
Set aside.
3 Brush each potato
shell inside and out with
the oil. Place on a
baking tray and bake a
further 40 minutes or
until the skins have
become very crisp.

4 Fill each skin with
prepared Filling and
sprinkle with Parmesan.
Place on baking tray
and bake 10 minutes
more or until cheese is
golden. Serve with salad
and crusty bread.
5 To make Filling:
Heat oil in medium
pan; add bacon. Cook
over medium high heat
until golden brown.
Add onion and garlic.
Cook until onion is
soft. Add to potato
mixture, stir in sour
cream, chives and
pepper, to taste.

Taramasalata

Preparation time:
  40 minutes
Cooking time:
  Nil
Serves 6

3 medium potatoes
  (690 g), peeled
  and chopped
2 small onions, finely
  chopped
2 tablespoons olive oil
⅓ cup lemon juice
2 tablespoons white
  wine vinegar
¼ cup water
100 g tarama (see Note)

1 Cook potatoes in
boiling water until just
tender; drain. Place in
food processor bowl with
the onion. Process for
30 seconds or until

Clockwise from top: Potato and Herb Fritters, Crispy Skins, Taramasalata.

mixture is smooth.
2 With the motor constantly operating, add the combined oil, lemon juice, vinegar and water. Process for 30 seconds or until all liquid is incorporated. Add the tarama. Process for 1 minute or until smooth. Transfer to a bowl. Cover, refrigerate.

Note: Tarama is smoked cod's roe; it is available in small jars or tubs from most delicatessens and quality supermarkets.

27

1 *For Spicy Potato Pastries:* Cook the potato until just tender. Drain; set aside.

2. Combine potato, lemon juice, coriander and mint with spices in pan.

3. Place 2 teaspoons of potato mixture in the centre of each square.

4. Brush the top of each pastry with egg; sprinkle with poppy seeds.

Spicy Potato Pastries

Preparation time:
  40 minutes
Cooking time:
  15 minutes
Serves 4 to 6

4 large potatoes (1.3 kg),
  peeled and cut into
  small cubes
30 g butter
1 clove garlic, crushed
2 teaspoons finely
  grated fresh ginger
1 medium onion, finely
  chopped
1 teaspoon turmeric
1 teaspoon garam
  masala
1 teaspoon ground
  cardamom
1 tablespoon lemon
  juice
1/4 cup chopped fresh
  coriander
1/4 cup chopped fresh
  mint

4 sheets ready
  rolled puff pastry
1 egg, lightly beaten
2 teaspoons poppy seeds

1 Preheat oven to moderate 180°C. Brush two 32 x 28 cm oven trays with melted butter or oil. Cook potato in boiling water until just tender. Drain, set aside.
2 Heat the butter in a medium pan; add garlic, ginger, onion, turmeric, garam masala and cardamom. Cook over medium high heat for 4 minutes or until onion is soft. Add potato, lemon juice, coriander and mint; stir gently to combine. Remove from heat and cool mixture to room temperature.
3 Cut each pastry sheet into nine even squares. Brush edges with beaten egg. Place 2 teaspoons of potato mixture in the

centre of each square, fold over to form a triangle and press the edges gently to seal.
4 Brush the top of each triangle with egg; sprinkle with poppy seeds. Place 2.5 cm apart on prepared trays. Bake for 15 minutes or until well risen and golden brown.

Note: Pastries can be cooked a day ahead. They can be frozen successfully for up to 4 weeks.

HINT
For an even livelier filling for Spicy Potato Pastries, add 1/2 teaspoon chilli powder or 2 teaspoons finely chopped, fresh red chilli. Always wear rubber gloves when handling fresh chillies and avoid touching your skin or eyes – chilli can burn.

Spicy Potato Pastries.

29

Potato and Salami Pikelets

Preparation time:
  25 minutes
Cooking time:
  8 minutes
Makes 18 to 20 pikelets

1/2 cup milk
1 teaspoon white
  vinegar
1/2 cup self-raising flour
1 teaspoon bicarbonate
  of soda
1/2 cup mashed potato
  (150 g raw potato)
2 eggs, lightly beaten
30 g butter, melted
50 g salami, finely
  chopped
30 g butter, extra
50 g sun-dried
  tomatoes, cut into
  fine strips,
  for garnish
fresh basil leaves, for
  garnish

1 Combine milk and vinegar in a small bowl and leave for 5 minutes. Sift flour and soda into medium mixing bowl. Make a well in the centre; add mashed potato, eggs and combined milk and vinegar. Stir with a wooden spoon until well combined.
2 Add melted butter and salami, stir gently until combined.

3 Heat extra butter in medium pan; spoon level tablespoonsful of the mixture into pan, about 2 cm apart.
4 Cook over medium heat 3 minutes each side or until golden. Serve warm garnished with sun-dried tomatoes and basil leaves.

Note: Pikelets are best eaten on the day they are made. They can be frozen for 4 weeks.

Tomato Potato Pot

Preparation time:
  30 minutes
Cooking time:
  25 minutes
Serves 4 to 6

15 g butter
1 large onion, chopped
1 clove garlic, crushed
4 medium tomatoes
  (500 g), sliced
2 medium potatoes
  (460 g), peeled
  and sliced
2 tablespoons chopped
  fresh chives or spring
  onions
1 tablespoon tomato
  paste
1 chicken stock cube,
  crumbled
1 teaspoon finely grated
  lemon rind
1/2 teaspoon ground
  thyme

1 bay leaf
4 cups water
freshly ground pepper
sour cream, to serve
fresh thyme sprigs, for
  garnish

1 Heat the butter in large pan; add onion and garlic. Cook over medium heat until onion is soft. Add tomato, potato, chives, tomato paste, stock cube, rind, thyme, bay leaf and water.
2 Bring to the boil, reduce heat and simmer, uncovered, until potato is tender, about 20 minutes. Remove from heat; discard bay leaf. Allow to cool.
3 Place the mixture in batches in a food processor bowl. Process for 30 seconds or until the mixture is smooth. Return to pan, season with pepper to taste; heat through. Serve topped with a little sour cream and garnished with thyme sprigs.

HINT
Potatoes are not grown from seed, but from the eyes of the potatoes themselves. Always store your potatoes, unwrapped, in a cool, dark, airy place. Avoid potatoes with a pronounced greenish tinge as they can be poisonous.

Tomato Potato Pot, Potato and Salami Pikelets.

Quick and Easy Fish and Potato Chowder

Preparation time:
  20 minutes
Cooking time:
  10 minutes
Serves 6

1 tablespoon olive oil
2 rashers bacon, finely
  chopped
1 large onion, chopped
2 x 440 g cans whole
  potatoes, drained,
  sliced
1½ cups chicken stock
1 bay leaf
½ teaspoon dried
  tarragon leaves
¼ teaspoon dried
  thyme leaves
freshly ground pepper
375 g white fish fillets,
  cubed
1½ cups milk

1 Heat oil in medium
pan; add bacon and
onion. Cook over
medium high heat until
golden. Add potato,
stock, bay leaf,
tarragon, thyme and
pepper to taste. Bring to
the boil, reduce heat
and simmer covered, for
5 minutes.
2 Add the fish; cook,
covered, for 3 minutes.
Add milk; heat through.
Discard bay leaf. Serve
garnished with chopped
parsley, if desired.

Belgian Potato Soup

Preparation time:
  25 minutes
Cooking time:
  20 minutes
Serves 4 to 6

30 g butter
4 medium onions,
  thinly sliced
250 g mushrooms, sliced
4 cups chicken stock
4 sprigs fresh parsley
1 bay leaf
1 sprig fresh thyme
4 medium potatoes
  (920 g), peeled
  and chopped
1 cup cream

1 Heat butter in a
medium pan over low
heat; add onion and
mushrooms. Cook gently
until onion is soft. Add
stock and herbs, bring to
the boil, add the potato.
Reduce heat, cook,
covered, 30 minutes or
until potato is tender.
Cool. Discard bay leaf
and thyme.
2 Place soup mixture in
batches in a food
processor bowl. Process
for 30 seconds or until
the mixture is smooth.
Return the soup to the
pan with the cream;
reheat gently.

Vichyssoise

Preparation time:
  25 minutes plus
  1 hour refrigeration
Cooking time:
  30 minutes
Serves 6

2 large leeks, chopped
2 medium potatoes
  (460 g), peeled
  and chopped
2 tablespoons chopped
  fresh chives
3 cups chicken stock
1 cup milk
½ cup cream
grated nutmeg

1 Place leek, potato,
chives and stock in a
large pan. Bring to the
boil, reduce heat.
Simmer, covered, until
vegetables are tender,
about 30 minutes. Add
milk. Allow to cool.
2 Place soup in batches
in food processor bowl.
Process 30 seconds or
until smooth. Transfer
to large mixing bowl;
stir in cream. Cover and
refrigerate 1 hour or
overnight. Serve
sprinkled with nutmeg.

Note: Traditionally
served chilled, this soup
can, however, be gently
reheated and served hot.

---

*Clockwise from top right: Belgian
Potato Soup, Vichyssoise, Quick and Easy Fish
and Potato Chowder.*

Main courses

The potato enhances traditional recipes as well as those with a contemporary slant. Irish Lamb and Potato Stew and Shepherd's Pie are both classic, cold-weather favourites. Croquettes are excellent when you want to make a little go a long way, and omelettes, casseroles, gnocchi and hamburgers are all enhanced by the useful potato. These delicious meals satisfy the heartiest appetites.

Irish Lamb and Potato Stew

Preparation time:
  25 minutes
Cooking time: 1 hour
  30 minutes
Serves 4 to 6

8 *medium potatoes*
  (1.8 kg), peeled
1 *kg lamb neck chops*
1/2 *teaspoon ground*
  pepper
4 *large onions, thickly*
  sliced
2 *cups chicken stock*
2 *bay leaves*
3/4 *cup finely chopped*
  fresh parsley

1 Thickly slice the potatoes. Trim meat of excess fat.

2 Arrange half the potato over the base of a deep, heavy-based pan. Add meat, pepper, onion and remaining potato. Pour the chicken stock over and add bay leaves.
3 Cover the pan with a tight-fitting lid and cook over low heat for 1 hour 30 minutes. Sprinkle with parsley just before serving.

Note: Lining the base of the pan with sliced potatoes is essential to this dish; they break down during cooking and thicken the stock, producing the traditional creamy sauce. This dish can be made 2 days ahead and refrigerated; it is unsuitable to freeze.

Potato-coated Meatloaf (page 36),
Irish Lamb and Potato Stew.

Potato-coated Meatloaf

Preparation time:
  50 minutes
Cooking time: 1 hour
  20 minutes
Serves 4 to 6

1 kg pork and veal
  mince
1 cup (60 g) fresh white
  or wholemeal
  breadcrumbs
1/2 cup evaporated milk
1 egg, lightly beaten
1/4 cup tomato sauce
1 tablespoon
  Worcestershire sauce
1 medium onion, finely
  chopped
1 tablespoon finely
  chopped fresh sage
4 rashers bacon, rind
  removed
3 hard-boiled eggs
2 cups mashed potato
  (600 g raw potato)
30 g melted butter

1 Preheat oven to
moderate 180°C. Brush
a 21 x 14 x 7 cm loaf
tin with melted butter
or oil.
2 Place the meat,
breadcrumbs, evaporated
milk, egg, sauces, onion
and sage in a large bowl;
mix well with your hands.
3 Line the surface of the
tin with bacon rashers.
Divide meat mixture
evenly into three; spread
one portion evenly over
base of bacon-lined tin.

Place the eggs down the
centre and pack the
remaining meat mixture
over and around them.
4 Bake for 1 hour or
until mixture shrinks
from sides of tin.
Remove from oven,
leave for 5 minutes;
pour off excess juices
from tin. Carefully turn
loaf out onto oven tray.
5 Spread the mashed
potato over loaf, brush
with melted butter.
Return loaf to oven and
bake for further
15 minutes or until
potato is golden brown.
6 Serve sliced meatloaf
with your favourite
pickle or chutney.

Note: Serve sliced, hot or
cold. Meatloaf can be
cooked a day ahead and
is good picnic fare that
is easy to transport. It is
not suitable for freezing.

Vegetable Pie

Preparation time:
  40 minutes plus
  30 minutes standing
Cooking time:
  20 minutes
Serves 4 to 6

Pastry
1 1/2 cups plain
  wholemeal flour
125 g butter, cubed
1 tablespoon iced water
1 egg yolk, lightly beaten
2 teaspoons lemon juice

Filling
30 g butter
1 small onion, finely
  chopped
6 spinach leaves,
  washed and chopped
1/2 teaspoon ground
  nutmeg
1 cup mashed potato
  (300 g raw potato)
1 cup mashed pumpkin
  (200 g)
2 large, firm tomatoes,
  sliced
1 cup grated Cheddar
  cheese

1 To make Pastry: Sift
flour into large mixing
bowl. Return husks to
bowl. Add butter. Using
fingertips, rub butter
into flour for 4 minutes
or until mixture is a
fine, crumbly texture.
Make a well in the
centre and mix in
combined water, egg
yolk and lemon juice
until mixture clings
together to form a ball.
2 Place on lightly
floured surface and
knead for 1 minute.
Cover with plastic wrap
and refrigerate for
30 minutes.
3 Preheat oven to
moderately hot 210°C.
Brush a deep, 20 cm pie
plate lightly with
melted butter or oil.
Roll pastry out between
2 sheets of greaseproof
paper on lightly floured
surface. Line prepared
plate with pastry, being
careful not to stretch

Vegetable Pie.

pastry. Trim the excess from edge using large, sharp knife. Chill for 10 minutes.
4 Line the pastry with greaseproof paper, fill with rice, dried peas or beans. Bake for 12 minutes. Remove paper, rice, peas or beans and continue to

bake for 15 minutes or until pastry is cooked and golden brown. Cool for 5 minutes.
5 To make Filling: Melt butter in a medium pan; add the onion. Cook over medium high heat for 2 minutes. Add the spinach and nutmeg, cover and cook until

the spinach is tender.
6 Spread the mashed potato over the base of the baked pie crust; top with spinach mixture, mashed pumpkin, tomato slices and cheese. Bake for about 20 minutes to heat thoroughly. Serve pie hot or cold.

Beef and Potato Curry

Preparation time:
  20 minutes
Cooking time: 1 hour
Serves 4 to 6

*750 g round or topside
  steak
1 tablespoon olive oil
3 large onions, chopped
4 cloves garlic,
  crushed
1 tablespoon finely
  grated fresh ginger
1 teaspoon chilli powder
2 teaspoons ground
  cardamom
2 teaspoons turmeric
1½ cups beef stock
6 large potatoes (2 kg),
  peeled and cubed*

1 Trim meat of excess
fat; cut into large cubes.
Heat oil in heavy-based
pan. Add meat in small
batches, cooking it over
medium high heat until
well browned; drain on
absorbent paper.
2 Add the onion, garlic
and ginger to pan and
cook 2 minutes. Add
chilli powder, cardamom
and turmeric; cook,
stirring constantly, for
2 minutes.
3 Return meat to pan
with stock; bring to the
boil. Reduce heat to a
simmer, cook, covered,
for 35 minutes. Add the
potato and cook,
uncovered, until tender.

Layered Potato and Chicken

Preparation time:
  40 minutes
Cooking time:
  20 minutes
Serves 4 to 6

*3 medium potatoes
  (690 g), peeled and
  thickly sliced
500 g orange sweet
  potato, peeled and
  thickly sliced
3 chicken breast fillets
1 cup water
½ cup dry white wine
2 bay leaves
1 strip of lemon rind
60 g butter
3 tablespoons plain flour
¾ cup milk
2 tablespoons
  mayonnaise
2 teaspoons prepared
  mild mustard
¼ cup lemon juice*

Topping
*⅔ cup fresh wholemeal
  breadcrumbs
⅓ cup grated Cheddar
  cheese
1 tablespoon chopped
  fresh chives*

1 Preheat oven to
moderate 180°C. Brush
a deep ovenproof dish
lightly with melted
butter. Boil potatoes
until just tender. Drain.

2 Place chicken in a
medium pan with water,
wine, bay leaves and
lemon rind. Bring to the
boil and simmer,
covered, for 10 minutes.
Remove the chicken and
set aside. Continue to
boil stock, uncovered,
until it has reduced to
1 cup. Discard bay
leaves. Cut each breast
into 6 slices.
3 Heat the butter in
medium pan, add flour.
Stir over low heat for
2 minutes or until flour
mixture is lightly
golden. Add the
reserved stock and milk
gradually to pan,
stirring until mixture is
smooth. Stir constantly
over medium heat for
5 minutes or until
mixture boils and
thickens; boil a further
1 minute. Remove from
heat. Leave the mixture
to cool for about
5 minutes. Stir in the
mayonnaise, mustard
and lemon juice.
4 Place half the potatoes
over base of dish, top
with chicken and finish
with remaining potatoes.
Pour sauce mixture
evenly over top. Sprinkle
on combined Topping
ingredients. Bake for
20 minutes or until
heated through. Serve at
once with a salad of
your choice.

*Layered Potato and Chicken (top), Beef and
Potato Curry (bottom).*

Salmon and Camembert Croquettes

Preparation time:
  40 minutes + 3 hours standing
Cooking time:
  5 minutes
Makes 16

3 large potatoes (1 kg), peeled and chopped
1 small onion, finely chopped
2 x 210 g cans pink salmon, drained and flaked
1 tablespoon chopped fresh parsley
2 teaspoons finely grated lemon rind
1/4 cup lemon juice
1 tablespoon vinegar
1 egg, lightly beaten
freshly ground pepper
60 g Camembert cheese, cubed
1/4 cup plain flour
ground pepper, extra

2 eggs, lightly beaten, extra (see Note)
1-1 1/2 cups (60-90 g) fresh white breadcrumbs
oil, for deep-frying

1 Cook potato in large pan of boiling water until just tender; drain and mash. Transfer to a large mixing bowl. Add onion, salmon, parsley, lemon rind and juice, vinegar, egg and pepper to taste. Stir to combine.
2 Divide mixture into 16 evenly sized portions. Form each portion into a sausage shape about 7 cm long, working a piece of Camembert into the centre of each one.
3 Combine flour and pepper on a sheet of greaseproof paper. Toss the croquettes in the seasoned flour; shake off the excess. Dip into beaten egg, then into

the crumbs to coat them evenly; shake off excess. Store, covered, in the refrigerator for 3 hours.
4 Heat oil in deep, heavy-based pan. Gently lower a few croquettes at a time into moderately hot oil. Cook over medium high heat for 5 minutes or until golden brown. Carefully remove from oil with tongs. Drain on absorbent paper, keep warm. Repeat with remaining croquettes. Serve as an entrée, an accompaniment or as a main meal with vegetables or salad.

Note: You can use one egg instead of two for coating, beating in a little milk to produce sufficient liquid. Croquettes may be prepared to the end of Step 3 and refrigerated for up to 2 days.

Salmon and Camembert Croquettes.

1. For Croquettes: Add the onion, salmon, parsley, rind, juice, vinegar, egg and pepper.

2. Form portions into sausage shapes, working in a small piece of Camembert.

3. Coat each croquette with flour, beaten egg and breadcrumbs; shake off excess.

4. Gently lower a few croquettes at a time into the moderately hot oil.

Spanish Omelette

Preparation time:
  20 minutes
Cooking time:
  20 minutes
Serves 4 to 6

2 tablespoons olive oil
1 large onion, thinly
  sliced
3 large potatoes (1 kg),
  peeled and cubed
1 small green capsicum,
  seeded and sliced
1 small red capsicum,
  seeded and sliced
3 rashers bacon, cut
  into small strips
100 g cabanossi, sliced
1 tablespoon olive oil,
  extra
8 eggs, lightly beaten
1/3 cup finely chopped
  chives

1 Heat oil in large,
heavy-based pan; add
the onion and potato.
Cook over medium heat
for 10 minutes or until
the potato is cooked
and golden brown.
Remove from the pan;
set aside.
2 Add capsicum, bacon
and cabanossi and cook
over medium heat for
5 minutes. Add extra oil
and the onion and potato
mixture and continue to
cook for 2 to 3 minutes,
mixing gently to combine.

3 Pour in eggs and
cook over medium heat
for 10 minutes or until
set. Brown the top
under a medium hot
grill. Sprinkle with
chives. Cut into wedges
and serve.

Note: Spanish Omelette
can be served hot or
cold accompanied by
green salad and crusty
bread. This recipe can
be varied to include
other seasonal
vegetables, herbs and
sausage of your choice.

Potato and Corn Slice

Preparation time:
  25 minutes
Cooking time:
  40 minutes
Serves 4 to 6

1/2 cup self-raising flour
2 cups mashed potato
  (600 g raw potato)
3 eggs, lightly beaten
1 x 310 g can creamed
  corn
1 tablespoon sweet
  chilli sauce
1 cup grated Cheddar
  cheese
1 large packet of corn
  chips
4 tomatoes, chopped
1 avocado, chopped
1 cup sour cream

*Spanish Omelette (top), Potato and Corn
Slice (bottom).*

1 Preheat oven to
moderate 180°C. Brush
a 25 x 15 x 5.5 cm loaf
tin with melted butter
or oil, line base and
sides with paper; grease
paper.
2 Sift flour into
medium mixing bowl.
Make a well in the
centre, stir in potato
and eggs until mixture
is well combined. Place
corn in small bowl; add
chilli, stir to combine.
3 Spread half of the
potato mixture evenly
over surface of prepared
tin. Top with the corn
mixture and spread
remaining potato
mixture on top.
4 Sprinkle on cheese.
Bake for 40 minutes or
until golden brown and
firm. Leave in tin for
15 minutes before
cutting into squares to
serve. Serve with the
corn chips, tomato,
avocado and a spoonful
of sour cream.

Note: This recipe is best
made on the day it is
required and is not
suitable for freezing.

HINT
Most of the valuable
vitamin C contained
in potatoes is stored
just under the skin.
Depending on the
potatoes used, peeling
is optional, even if it's
specified in the recipe.

Potato and Cheese Hamburgers
Preparation time:
  30 minutes
Cooking time:
  10 minutes
Serves 4 to 6

*1 large eggplant, cut
  into 6 to 8 rounds*
*1 cup mashed potato
  (300 g raw potato)*
500 g minced beef
*1/4 cup freshly grated
  Parmesan cheese*
*1 medium onion, finely
  chopped*
*1/3 cup finely chopped
  fresh basil*
1 egg, lightly beaten
*1 tablespoon tomato
  paste*
*basil leaves, extra, for
  garnish*

1 Place eggplant in
colander, sprinkle with
salt and leave for
20 minutes. Rinse in
cold water and pat dry.
2 Place potato, minced
beef, cheese, onion,
basil, egg and tomato
paste in a large bowl.
Using your hands, mix
until well combined.
With wetted hands,
shape into 6 or 8 even,
round hamburgers.
3 Place the prepared
hamburgers and
eggplant slices on a
cold, lightly oiled grill.
Cook under medium
heat for 10 minutes,

turning once, or until
cooked and tender.
4 Serve each hamburger
on a slice of the
eggplant; garnish with a
few basil leaves.

Note: Hamburgers can
be prepared up to the
grilling stage a day
ahead. Store, covered, in
the refrigerator.
Uncooked hamburgers
may be frozen for
up to 4 weeks. For a
variation, use tomato or
pineapple slices as the
base for the burgers
instead of the eggplant.

Potato, Ham and Leek Casserole
Preparation time:
  15 minutes
Cooking time:
  50 minutes
Serves 4 to 6

*1 medium orange sweet
  potato (230 g), peeled*
*4 medium potatoes
  (920 g), peeled*
1 medium leek
1 tablespoon oil
*100 g ham or bacon,
  chopped*
*2 tablespoons plain
  flour*
1 1/4 cups cream
3/4 cup milk
*2 teaspoons chicken
  stock powder*
ground white pepper
*1/4 cup finely grated
  Parmesan cheese*

Potato, Ham and Leek Casserole.

1 Preheat oven to moderate 180°C. Finely slice potatoes. Wash leek thoroughly and finely slice, including 3 cm of the green part.
2 Heat oil in pan and cook leek for about 5 minutes. Add ham and continue cooking for 3 minutes. Sprinkle the flour over and stir to combine.

3 Layer the potatoes, alternating them with the cooked leek and ham mixture, in a lightly greased, shallow casserole or baking dish.
4 Combine the cream and milk in a small pan and heat gently; add chicken stock powder and season with pepper to taste. Pour over the potatoes. Bake for

50 minutes or until the potatoes are tender. Sprinkle with Parmesan cheese. Serve at once.

Note: Slice the potatoes thinly and evenly so that they cook evenly. Some food processors feature adjustable slicing discs. Adjust the disc so that the slices are about 2 mm thick.

1. For Gnocchi: Add flour, butter, Parmesan and pepper to potato, mix well.

2. Form into small rounds, indent lightly with the prongs of a fork to shape.

Creamy Blue Cheese Gnocchi

Preparation time:
  40 minutes
Cooking time:
  10 minutes
Serves 4 to 6

3 medium potatoes
  (690 g), peeled
  and chopped
2 cups plain flour
30 g butter, melted
1/4 cup grated Parmesan
  cheese
freshly ground pepper

Sauce
60 g butter
2 tablespoons plain
  flour
2 cups milk
1/2 teaspoon mustard
  powder
freshly ground pepper
125 g Blue Castello
  cheese, crumbled
3 spring onions, chopped

1 Cook potato in large pan of boiling water until just tender; drain and mash. Transfer to large mixing bowl. Add sifted flour, butter, Parmesan and pepper to taste. Mix until well combined. Turn onto a lightly floured surface. Knead for 4 minutes or until smooth.
2 Divide dough evenly into 2.5 cm pieces. Form into small rounds. Indent with fingertips or fork prongs to shape.
3 Heat a large pan of water until boiling. Gently lower batches of gnocchi into the boiling water and cook for 5 minutes or until gnocchi float to the top. Drain and keep warm.
4 To make Sauce: Heat butter in a medium pan; add flour. Stir over low heat until flour mixture is lightly golden. Add milk gradually to pan,

stirring until mixture is smooth. Stir constantly over medium heat for 2 minutes or until mixture boils and thickens; boil further 1 minute. Add mustard, pepper to taste, cheese and spring onions, stirring until cheese has melted. Pour sauce over the gnocchi.
Serve at once with a crisp green salad and crusty bread.

Note: Gnocchi is also delicious topped with fresh tomato sauce.

HINT
Don't store potatoes in the refrigerator; their starch will turn into sugar and the resultant dish will taste peculiarly sweet. However, the sugar will return to starch if the potatoes are left at room temperature for a few days.

Creamy Blue Cheese Gnocchi.

3. Cook gnocchi for about 5 minutes or until they float to the surface.

4. Add mustard, pepper, crumbled cheese and spring onions to sauce.

47

Potatoes Moussaka

Preparation time:
40 minutes
Cooking time:
45 minutes
Serves 6

60 g butter
1/2 cup plain flour
2 cups milk
1/4 teaspoon cayenne
  pepper
1/4 teaspoon ground
  nutmeg
1 tablespoon olive oil
2 large onions, thinly
  sliced
2-2 1/2 cups finely
  chopped cooked lamb
2 cloves garlic, crushed
1 x 440 g can tomatoes,
  drained, crushed, juice
  reserved
1 bay leaf
freshly ground pepper
4 medium potatoes
  (920 g), peeled
  and chopped
2 tablespoons olive oil
4 medium potatoes
  (920 g), peeled, extra
1 cup grated Cheddar
  cheese

1 Preheat oven to
moderate 180°C.
2 Heat butter in large
pan; add sifted flour.
Stir over low heat for
2 minutes or until the
flour mixture is lightly
golden. Add the milk

gradually to the pan,
stirring until mixture is
smooth. Add cayenne
pepper and nutmeg. Stir
constantly over medium
heat 2 minutes or until
mixture boils and
thickens; boil 1 minute
more. Take pan off heat.
3 Heat the oil in a
heavy-based pan; add
the onion. Cook over
medium high heat until
onion is soft. Add lamb
and garlic, cook,
stirring, 2 to 3 minutes.
Add tomatoes and
4 tablespoons of
reserved liquid, bay leaf
and pepper to taste.
Simmer, uncovered, for
5 minutes.
4 Cook potato in large
pan of boiling water
until just tender; drain
and mash.
5 Cut extra potatoes
into 2 mm slices. Heat
oil in heavy-based pan;
add potato slices. Cook
over medium high heat
2 minutes or until
golden. Remove and
drain on absorbent
paper. Layer potato
slices and meat mixture
in a deep ovenproof
dish; spread mashed
potato over top.
6 Spoon over prepared
sauce, sprinkle with
cheese and bake
45 minutes until heated
through and cheese
topping has melted.

Italian Fish and Potato Stew

Preparation time:
30 minutes
Cooking time:
20 minutes
Serves 4 to 6

2 tablespoons olive oil
2 medium onions, sliced
3 cloves garlic, crushed
1 small red capsicum,
  seeded and chopped
1 small green capsicum,
  seeded and chopped
1/4 cup finely chopped
  fresh rosemary
1/4 cup finely chopped
  fresh parsley
1 cup tomato purée
1/2 cup dry white wine
6 small potatoes
  (840 g), quartered
4 medium white fish
  fillets (about 500 g),
  cut into 2 cm cubes
1 lemon, sliced

1 Heat oil in large pan;
add onion, garlic and
capsicum. Cook over
medium heat for
10 minutes or until soft
and golden. Add
rosemary, parsley,
tomato purée and white
wine; bring to the boil,
add the potato and
simmer, covered, until
potato is just tender.
2 Add fish and simmer,
uncovered, for 8 minutes
or until fish is cooked.
Serve immediately
garnished with lemon.

---

*Potatoes Moussaka (top), Italian Fish and
Potato Stew (bottom).*

49

Fish and Potato Bake

Preparation time:
45 minutes
Cooking time:
30 minutes
Serves 4

1 x 750 g *whole bream,*
cleaned and scaled
2 *cups milk*
half a lemon, sliced
1 *bay leaf*
1/2 *teaspoon black*
peppercorns
1 *small onion, quartered*
1 *small carrot, thickly*
sliced
1 *sprig fresh parsley*
30 g *butter*
2 *medium onions,*
extra, thinly sliced
30 g *butter, extra*
2 *tablespoons plain flour*
2 *hard-boiled eggs,*
chopped
4 *medium potatoes*
(920 g), peeled and
thinly sliced
1/4 *cup grated Cheddar*
cheese
2 *tablespoons fresh*
breadcrumbs

1 Preheat oven to
moderate 180°C.
Remove head from fish
and discard. Place fish
in a large, shallow pan.
Pour over milk, add
lemon slices, bay leaf,
peppercorns, onion,
carrot and parsley. Heat
to barely simmering;
cook for 5 minutes. Cool.

2 Remove fish from
pan, reserve liquid and
strain. Remove bones
and skin from fish and
discard. Flake flesh and
set aside.
3 Heat butter in a
small pan; add extra
onion. Cook over
medium high heat for
3 minutes or until soft;
set aside.
4 Heat extra butter in
pan; add flour. Stir over
low heat 2 minutes or
until flour mixture is
lightly golden. Add the
reserved fish liquid
gradually to pan,
stirring until mixture is
smooth. Stir constantly
over medium heat for
2 minutes or until the
mixture boils and
thickens, boil further
1 minute; remove from
heat. Stir in fish.
5 Spread onion over
base of shallow,
ovenproof dish. Top
with fish mixture and
eggs. Pour over half the
prepared sauce.
Arrange potato slices
neatly over fish mixture
to completely cover.
Pour over remaining
sauce. Top with
combined cheese and
breadcrumbs. Bake for
30 minutes or until the
topping is golden
brown. Serve with salad.

Note: Substitute 500 g
smoked haddock for
the bream, or use a
mixture of seafood.

Shepherd's Pie

Preparation time:
45 minutes
Cooking time:
15 minutes
Serves 6

1 *tablespoon olive oil*
2 *small onions, chopped*
500 g *lamb mince*
1 *tablespoon plain flour*
1 x 440 g *can tomatoes,*
drained, juice reserved
1 *beef stock cube,*
crumbled
2 *teaspoons*
Worcestershire sauce
1/2 *cup frozen peas*
2 *medium carrots,*
finely chopped
4 *large potatoes*
(1.3 kg), peeled
and chopped
1/4 *cup sour cream*
freshly ground pepper

1 Preheat oven to
moderate 180°C. Heat
oil in a heavy-based
pan; add onion. Cook
over medium high heat
until soft. Add mince.
Cook 10 minutes or
until well browned and
almost all liquid has
evaporated. Use a fork
to break up any lumps
of mince as it cooks.
2 Blend flour with a
little reserved tomato
juice until smooth. Add
sufficient water to
remaining tomato juice
to make up 1 cup.
Blend into the flour

Shepherd's Pie (top), Fish and Potato Bake (bottom).

mixture with crumbled stock cube.
3 Gradually add liquid to mince mixture, stirring constantly over medium high heat. Add the tomatoes, Worcestershire sauce, peas and carrots. Mix well. Bring to the boil and simmer, covered, for 25 minutes or until

the meat is tender.
4 Cook the potato in a large pan of boiling water until tender. Drain, mash well. Blend in sour cream and pepper to taste until smooth. Place the mince mixture in a deep, ovenproof dish. Top with potato, using a fork to spread it evenly.

Bake for 15 minutes or until the top is golden brown. Serve with a salad or with vegetables of your choice.

Note: Shepherd's Pie can also be made with leftover lamb from a roast. Cottage Pie is a similar dish, but must be made with beef.

Breads and baking

B aking breads and cakes is one of the most satisfying of culinary pursuits, and the aroma of these home-made goodies certainly takes some beating.

Once again, the potato surprises with its versatility, adding a unique texture to baked items. The fashion for a cosmopolitan range of breads is now at its height; try our intriguing Olive Potato Bread with a bowl of soup, or, for something a little different for morning tea, serve the Currant Coconut Round or a slice of cream-filled Potato Almond Torte.

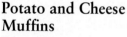

Potato and Cheese Muffins

Preparation time:
  15 minutes
Cooking time:
  10 minutes
Makes 32 muffins

2 cups self-raising
  flour
2¾ cups peeled, grated
  potato (460 g)
½ cup grated Cheddar
  cheese
2 rashers bacon, finely
  chopped
1 egg, lightly beaten
1 tablespoon olive oil
1 cup milk

1 Preheat oven to moderate 180°C. Brush bases of deep ¼ cup patty tins lightly with melted butter or oil.
2 Sift flour into large mixing bowl. Add the potato, cheese and bacon. Make a well in the centre. Add the combined egg, olive oil and milk. Stir with a fork until just combined; do not overbeat the mixture.
3 Spoon level tablespoonfuls of the mixture into tins. Bake for 10 minutes, or until well risen and golden.
4 Leave 2 minutes in tins before turning onto wire rack to cool.

Clockwise from top right: Olive Potato Bread (page 55), Potato and Tomato Scones (page 54), Potato and Cheese Muffins.

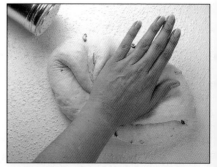

1. *For Olive Potato Bread: Add potato to flour, olives and yeast mixture.*

2. *Knead dough on a lightly floured surface for 4 minutes or until smooth.*

Potato and Tomato Scones

Preparation time:
  20 minutes
Cooking time:
  10 minutes
Makes 12

1½ *cups self-raising flour*
½ *cup mashed potato (150 g raw potato)*
¼ *teaspoon bicarbonate of soda*
2 *tablespoons grated Parmesan cheese*
2 *eggs, lightly beaten*
2 *tablespoons chopped sun-dried tomatoes*
1 *tablespoon grated Parmesan cheese, extra*

1 Preheat oven to moderate 180°C. Brush base of 32 x 28 cm scone tray lightly with melted butter or oil. Coat with flour; shake off excess.
2 Combine all the ingredients except extra Parmesan in a food processor bowl. Using the pulse action, process for 15 seconds or until the mixture comes together.

3 Turn mixture onto floured surface. Knead lightly for about 2 minutes or until smooth. Pat dough out to 2 cm thickness; cut into rounds with a 4 cm cutter which has been dipped in flour.
4 Place scones close together on tray. Brush tops with extra milk, sprinkle with cheese. Bake for 10 to 15 minutes or until scones are well risen and golden. Serve hot with butter.

Note: Scones are best eaten on the day they are baked. They can be frozen successfully for up to 4 weeks. Mashed potato is best used warm, not hot. Do not add butter or milk to the potato when mashing it because this will soften it and make it the incorrect consistency for bread and cake baking.

HINT

The success of muffin making relies on minimum mixing. A fork only should be used for mixing and the mixture should be stirred quickly and lightly. The tins should be only three-quarters full; avoid topping up tins with any spare mixture. Muffins should have a rough, uneven appearance. They are best served on the day that they are baked. However, they can be frozen successfully; store them in a freezer container, label and freeze for a maximum of 4 weeks.

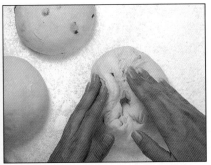

3. *Knead each portion of the dough for 2 minutes and shape into a round.*

4. *Top each recess with extra sliced olives and drizzle with olive oil.*

Olive Potato Bread

Preparation time: 1 hour
Cooking time:
  15 minutes
Makes 3 x 15 cm rounds

1 x 7 g sachet dried
  yeast
1 teaspoon caster sugar
3 cups plain flour
1¼ cups warm water
1 cup mashed potato
  (300 g raw potato)
½ cup black olives,
  sliced
½ cup black olives,
  extra, sliced
1 tablespoon olive oil,
  extra

1 Preheat oven to moderately hot 210°C. Brush a 32 x 28 cm oven tray with melted butter or oil.
2 Combine yeast, sugar and 2 tablespoons of flour in a medium mixing bowl. Gradually add water; blend until smooth. Leave, covered with plastic wrap, in a warm place for about 10 minutes or until it is foamy.
3 Sift remaining flour into large mixing bowl. Make a well in the centre, add potato, olives and yeast mixture. Using a knife, mix to a soft dough. Turn the dough onto lightly floured surface; knead for about 4 minutes or until smooth. Shape dough into a ball, place in a large, lightly oiled mixing bowl. Leave, covered with plastic wrap, in warm place for 15 minutes or until it is well risen.
4 Knead the dough again for 5 minutes or until smooth. Divide the dough into 3 pieces. Knead one portion at a time on a lightly floured surface for 2 minutes and shape each portion into a ball.

5 Place the dough on prepared oven tray. Press dough down in centre to form a shallow recess; fill with extra olives and drizzle with oil. Bake for 15 to 20 minutes or until well browned and cooked through. Leave for 5 minutes on tray before transferring to a wire rack to cool.

Note: Olive Potato Bread is best eaten on the day baked. It can be frozen successfully for up to 4 weeks.

HINT
1 cup of mashed potato weighs 240 g and is made from 300 g raw potato. When estimating the amount of potatoes you will need for a specific number of people, allow 1½ medium potatoes (345 g) per person.

Potato Soda Bread

Preparation time:
  15 minutes
Cooking time:
  25 minutes
Makes 1 x 20 cm round

2 cups wholemeal plain
  flour
1½ cups plain flour
2 teaspoons
  bicarbonate of soda
2 teaspoons cream of
  tartar
60 g butter, chopped
½ cup rolled oats
1 cup mashed potato
  (300 g raw potato)
1 cup skim milk
plain flour, extra, for
  dusting

1 Preheat oven to
moderate 180°C. Brush
a 32 x 28 cm scone tray
with melted butter, dust
lightly with flour.
2 Sift flours, soda and
cream of tartar into
large mixing bowl. Add
chopped butter.
3 Using fingertips, rub
butter into flour for
3 minutes or until the
mixture is a fine,
crumbly texture. Add
the rolled oats and
potato, stir to combine.
4 Add milk to bowl
and stir with a knife to
form a soft dough. Turn
onto a lightly floured
surface and knead
lightly for about 2 to
3 minutes or until

smooth. Shape into ball
and place on prepared
tray. Flatten into a
round 3 cm thick. Cut
the round into quarters,
dust lightly with extra
plain flour.
5 Bake for 25 minutes
until well risen and
golden brown or until
skewer comes out clean
when inserted in the
centre of bread. Turn
onto a wire rack. Serve
warm with butter.

Cheesy Potato Biscuits

Preparation time:
  25 minutes
Cooking time:
  10 minutes
Makes 10

1 cup plain flour
⅓ cup mashed potato
  (100 g raw potato)
2 tablespoons grated
  Parmesan cheese
1 tablespoon milk
1 egg, lightly beaten
¼ teaspoon mustard
  powder
pinch of cayenne pepper
½ cup grated Cheddar
  cheese
⅓ cup rolled oats

1 Preheat oven to
moderately hot 210°C.
Brush an oven tray with
melted butter or oil.
2 Combine the sifted
flour, potato, Parmesan,
milk, egg, mustard

and cayenne in a large
mixing bowl. Stir with
a wooden spoon until
well combined.
3 With well-floured
hands, shape heaped
tablespoons of mixture
into balls. Roll biscuit
mixture in combined
cheese and oats. Press
balls flat to make circles
about 5 cm in diameter.
4 Place biscuits on
prepared tray. Bake for
10 minutes, or until
slightly crisp and
golden. Place on a wire
rack to cool.

Potato Bread

Preparation time:
  15 minutes
Cooking time:
  35 minutes
Makes 1 x 20 cm round

2 cups plain flour
1 cup self-raising flour
½ teaspoon salt
1 teaspoon bicarbonate
  of soda
30 g butter, chopped
¼ teaspoon caster sugar
1 cup mashed potato
  (300 g raw potato)
⅔ cup buttermilk
1 egg, lightly beaten
⅔ cup buttermilk, extra

1 Preheat oven to
moderate 180°C. Brush
a deep, 20 cm sandwich
tin with melted butter or
oil. Line base and side
with paper; grease paper.

Clockwise from top right: Potato Bread, Potato Soda Bread and Cheesy Potato Biscuits.

2 Sift the flours, salt and bicarbonate of soda in a large mixing bowl; add butter and sugar. Using fingertips, rub the butter into the flour for 3 minutes or until the mixture is a fine, crumbly texture. Add potato; mix thoroughly. **3** Add the combined buttermilk and egg to bowl. Add enough of the extra buttermilk to form a soft dough. Spread dough into tin. **4** Using a sharp knife, score the top of the loaf into quarters. Bake for 35 minutes. Turn loaf onto a wire rack, brush the top with a little melted butter and leave to cool.

57

Chocolate Cinnamon Cake

Preparation time:
  25 minutes
Cooking time:
  45 minutes
Makes 1 x 20 cm cake

1/3 cup milk
1 teaspoon malt vinegar
125 g butter
1/2 cup caster sugar
2 eggs, lightly beaten
1/2 cup chopped pecans
1 cup warm mashed
  potato (300 g raw
  potato)
1 1/2 cups self-raising
  flour
3 tablespoons cocoa
  powder
2 teaspoons ground
  cinnamon

Frosting
1 cup icing sugar
1/2 teaspoon ground
  cinnamon
60 g softened butter
1 tablespoon hot water
extra pecans, for topping

1 Preheat oven to
moderate 180°C. Brush
a deep, 20 cm square
cake tin with melted
butter or oil. Line base
and side with paper;
grease paper. Combine
milk and vinegar, set
aside (see Note).
2 Using electric beaters,

beat butter and sugar in
a small mixing bowl
until light and creamy.
Add the eggs gradually,
beating thoroughly
after each addition.
3 Transfer the mixture
to large mixing bowl;
add pecans and mashed
potato. Using a metal
spoon, fold in the sifted
dry ingredients
alternately with milk
mixture. Stir until just
combined and mixture
is almost smooth.
4 Spoon mixture into
prepared tin; smooth
surface. Bake for
45 minutes or until
skewer comes out clean
when inserted in centre
of cake. Leave cake in
tin for 5 minutes before
turning onto wire rack
to cool. Spread the top
of cake with Frosting.
Sprinkle with the
extra pecans.
5 To make Frosting:
Combine sifted icing
sugar, cinnamon, butter
and hot water in small
bowl; beat until
mixture is combined
and creamy.

Note: Leave milk and
vinegar at room
temperature for at least
10 minutes or until
milk thickens slightly.
This soured milk will
help give the cake its
desired texture.

Currant Coconut Round

Preparation time:
  20 minutes
Cooking time:
  45 minutes
Makes 1 x 17 cm cake

1 1/2 cups self-raising
  flour
1/2 cup desiccated
  coconut
1/2 cup caster sugar
1 cup currants
1/2 cup mashed potato
  (150 g raw potato)
1/2 cup milk

1 Preheat oven to
moderate 180°C. Brush
a deep, 17 cm round
cake tin with melted
butter or oil. Line base
and side with paper;
grease paper.
2 Sift flour into large
mixing bowl. Add
coconut, sugar and
currants. Make a well
in the centre. Add
potato and milk to
combined ingredients.
Stir with a wooden
spoon until mixture is
well combined; do not
overbeat.
3 Spoon mixture into
prepared tin. Bake for
45 minutes or until
skewer comes out clean
when inserted in centre
of cake. Leave the cake
in the tin 5 minutes
before turning it onto a
wire rack to cool.

*Chocolate Cinnamon Cake (top), Currant
Coconut Round (bottom).*

Poppy Seed Loaf

Preparation time:
 15 minutes
Cooking time:
 50 minutes
Makes 1 loaf

*2½ cups self-raising
 flour
¼ cup caster sugar
¼ cup poppy seeds
6 cups peeled, grated
 potato (1 kg)
185 g butter, melted
 and cooled
2 eggs, lightly beaten
1 teaspoon poppy
 seeds, extra*

1 Preheat oven to
moderate 180°C. Brush
a 21 x 14 x 7 cm loaf
tin with melted butter
or oil. Line the base
and sides with paper;
grease paper.
2 Sift flour into large
mixing bowl. Add
sugar, poppy seeds and
potato. Make a well in
the centre. Add butter
and eggs. Stir with a
wooden spoon until just
combined; do not
overbeat.
3 Spoon mixture into
prepared tin; smooth
surface, sprinkle with
extra poppy seeds. Bake
for 50 minutes or until
skewer comes out clean
when inserted in centre
of loaf. Leave loaf in tin
for 3 minutes before
turning it onto a wire
rack to cool.

Note: Loaf will keep
refrigerated for 4 days.
It can also be frozen
successfully for up to
4 weeks. Because this
loaf contains only a
small amount of sugar,
it is an excellent
accompaniment to a
cheese and/or fruit
platter. Also, serve it
thinly sliced and
buttered for morning or
afternoon tea.

Potato Almond Torte

Preparation time:
 25 minutes
Cooking time:
 35 minutes
Makes 1 x 20 cm cake

*4 eggs, lightly beaten
⅔ cup caster sugar
2 teaspoons grated
 lemon rind
1 tablespoon lemon
 juice
⅓ cup self-raising flour
1 tablespoon rice flour
½ cup ground almonds
½ cup mashed potato
 (150 g raw potato)
whipped cream
 (optional)
icing sugar (optional)*

1 Preheat oven to
moderate 180°C. Brush
a deep, 20 cm round
cake tin with melted
butter or oil. Line base
with paper; grease
paper. Dust tin lightly
with flour, shake off
excess.
2 Place eggs and sugar
in a large, dry mixing
bowl. Using electric

*Potato Almond Torte (top), Poppy
Seed Loaf (bottom).*

beaters, beat until mixture is thick, pale yellow and glossy.

3 Using a metal spoon, fold in the lemon rind, juice, sifted flours, the almonds and the potato quickly and lightly.

4 Spread the mixture evenly into prepared tin. Bake for 35 minutes or until sponge is lightly golden and has shrunk from the side of the tin. Leave sponge in tin for 5 minutes before turning onto a wire rack to cool.

Either serve plain for afternoon tea or split and filled with lightly whipped cream if serving for dessert. Dust with sifted icing sugar.

Note: Potato Almond Torte will keep for up to 3 days in the refrigerator. It can also be frozen successfully for up to 4 weeks. Make a day ahead and refrigerate, unfilled, to allow the flavours to thoroughly develop. Fill with whipped cream just before serving.

Date and Ginger Loaf

Preparation time:
  25 minutes
Cooking time:
  45 minutes
Makes 1 loaf

125 g butter
½ cup soft brown sugar
2 eggs, lightly beaten
¾ cup dates, chopped
¾ cup peeled, grated
  potato (125 g)
1¼ cups self-raising
  flour
2 teaspoons ground
  ginger
¼ cup orange juice
¼ cup milk

1 Preheat oven to moderate 180°C. Brush a 21 x 14 x 7 cm loaf tin with melted butter or oil. Line the base and sides with paper; grease paper.
2 Using electric beaters, beat butter and sugar in small mixing bowl until light and creamy. Add eggs gradually, beating thoroughly after each addition.
3 Transfer mixture to large mixing bowl; add dates and potato. Using a metal spoon, fold in sifted flour and ginger alternately with liquids. Stir until just combined and the mixture is almost smooth.
4 Spoon mixture into prepared tin; smooth surface. Bake for 45 minutes or until skewer comes out clean when inserted in centre of cake. Leave cake in tin for 5 minutes before turning onto wire rack to cool.

Note: Cake will keep refrigerated for up to 3 days. It can be frozen successfully for up to 4 weeks. Raisins or dried apricots can be used in place of dates.

Apricot Flan

Preparation time:
  40 minutes
Cooking time:
  20 minutes
Makes 1 x 23 cm flan

1¼ cups plain flour
½ cup mashed potato
  (150 g raw potato)
60 g butter, softened
⅓ cup caster sugar
2 egg yolks, lightly
  beaten
2 x 425 g cans apricot
  halves, well drained

Glaze
1 cup apricot jam
3 tablespoons water
1 tablespoon lemon juice

1 Preheat oven to moderately hot 210°C. Brush a 23 cm flan tin with melted butter.
2 Sift flour into a large mixing bowl, make a well in the centre; add potato, butter, sugar and egg yolks. Using your fingers, gradually incorporate flour into potato mixture. Knead gently to form a ball. Place, covered with plastic wrap, in refrigerator 30 minutes.
3 Roll pastry to fit flan tin between two sheets of greaseproof paper on a lightly floured surface. Line flan tin with pastry, being careful not to stretch pastry. Mould together any tears in pastry with fingers. Remove excess pastry by pressing rolling pin across edge. Refrigerate for 10 minutes.
4 Cover pastry with a piece of greaseproof paper, cover paper with rice, dried peas or beans. Bake for 10 minutes; remove rice, peas or beans and paper. Reduce oven to moderate 180°C and continue to cook for 10 minutes or until pastry is golden brown and crisp. Cool pastry case before using.
5 Brush pastry case with a little warm glaze. Place apricots cut-side-down in pastry case. Spoon over remaining warm glaze. Leave 1 hour; serve.
6 To prepare Glaze: Place jam, water and

Apricot Flan and Date and Ginger Loaf.

lemon juice in a small pan and stir over a low heat for 5 minutes. Pour mixture through a fine sieve, return to pan and cook, stirring, for 3 minutes. Cool Glaze to room temperature.

Note: Pastry case can be made a day ahead. Baked pastry case can be frozen successfully for up to 4 weeks. Finished Apricot Flan will keep, refrigerated, for up to 2 days.

HINT
Any fruity jam can be used for a glaze; most will need to be sieved. Add a little liqueur of your choice in place of lemon juice.

Index